I Write Letters in my Thoughts

MONA KHALIL

ISBN: 978-1-4834-6865-5 (sc)
ISBN: 978-1-4834-6864-8 (e)

Library of Congress Control Number: 2017906260

Lulu Publishing Services rev. date: 05/16/2017

CONTENTS

FOREWORD

"Dicen los científicos que estamos hechos de átomos, pero a mí me dijo un pajarito que estamos hechos de historias." – Eduardo Galeano

"Scientists say we are made up of atoms, but a little birdie told me that we are made up of stories." – Eduardo Galeano

Growing up as a son of Guatemalan and Mexican immigrant parents in South Central Los Angeles I realized there was a complicated relationship we were supposed to have to stories. I spent a lot of my childhood in my and other family members' homes. Most of my close family was Central American and I remember the atmosphere always being loud. Stories being shared about who did what, when, and to who. There were many sardonic quips at other folks' expenses and stories about work or some family drama that everyone had a take on. The flipside to this boisterous cultural connection to tales was that as children we were often expected to be quiet, remain silent. "Don't share too much" or more appropriately "La ropa sucia se lava en casa (dirty clothes are washed in house)."

It's speaking into and about that silence that makes *I Write Letters in my Thoughts* by Mona Khalil so powerful. The words in this work enliven memories and experiences that often remain muted for brown youth and adults left to navigate a gauntlet in the United States. Khalil captures what it means to grow up in complex and vexed worlds that present impossible expectations. *I Write Letters in my Thoughts* is a synoptic view into one person's journey through love, life, and ultimately towards liberation. This project is a testament to the power of storytelling as a historic healing method for communities who are often told to be quiet and patient. *I Write Letters in my Thoughts* allows us to realize that we are enough and that enough is enough; suffering is not our destiny, love is not impossible, and freedom is what we make it.

- Alex Villalpando
South Los Angeles
April 29th, 2017
25th Anniversary LA Uprising

ACKNOWLEDGEMENTS

To my grandmother, mother, and little sister.
Thank you, Warsan Shire.

INTRODUCTION

Since childhood I have needed an outlet I can trust. Writing has been my constant. Pen to paper is an intimate way of learning about myself and analyzing my surroundings.

I enjoy the creative process of expressing emotions. Experiencing the art that women of color create, by being honest with themselves heals and inspires me.

As a result of oppression and socioeconomic marginalization we experience as a community, I write to heal women. I want my poetry to take them on a journey.

PROLOGUE

Beauty is in the details.
Be worth my time.

Strength is in
How much I
Bounce off me.

IDENTITY

منى | **Mona**

Name dipped in mango,
Taste of fresh Moroccan mint.
Egyptian blood,
Guyanese culture.
Arab with a Caribbean vibe.

منى is wish.
خليل is friend.
الحب permanently written on my back
From right to left—
The love.

Rooted across ancestry,
Paisley tattoo on my hand.
I am love and freedom intertwined.

منى خليل

Mirror

She studies herself
Surrounded by people
Who love her.

Hated by people
Who see her secure
In her skin.

Expression

The emotions we first experience
With our parents shape us.

Internally configured
As a youngin',
Skills that have
Stayed with me.

I write obsessively,
Confessing my vulnerability.
My outlet is reflection.

FAMILY

منى خليل

Daughter

She wishes she knew
How her parents felt
The first time
They held her.

Did they promise to provide for her?
Say they would prioritize her above their needs?
They would consider her when making decisions?

An abandoned child
Senses before they speak.
She learned to lift her voice.
She still struggles.

She wrestles with attachment.

Lessons

Great grandparents before
They were parents.

What did you learn
From your grandmother
Who vanished?

Same woman who gives
What she does not have.

How did your mother cherish you—
Sweet notes, manipulation,
Borrowed money unreturned,
And no authority?

Same woman who gave up
Everything to keep you.

What did you learn
When he used
Authority
To mold you?

Same man who
Taught you life and death
Reside in the same breath.

Where did the voices
In your head
Carry you?

You were
A quiet child.

منى خليل

Wedding Cakes

Los Angeles magic.
Her mother was the first in the family
To marry outside her world.

Arduous marriage.
She held the family down,
Trying to bring heaven
To hell on earth.
She made it to seven.

Egregious divorce
Then entertained
Plans of taking him back.
He made her believe.

Until he returned
Remarried, birth of
Stepmother and sister.
She was twelve.

Her mother divorced
Her father twice.
She reappeared in Queens, New York,
Remarried to a baptized Muslim.
She was eight.

As her family grows
They represent atheism and all faiths:
Jewish, Hindu, Muslim, Christian,
Mixes of cultures and religions.

Know the
Power of boundaries,
Power of distance,
Power of love.

منى خليل

OG Bad***

Before I turned to
Strong black women,
There was my mother.

Fierce as ****
Made from her cloth,
She was my first model.

Vigorous brown skin.
My rebel.
My queen.
We endured trauma.

When I disengaged,
She struggled.

She tapped out
In living form.

I have to remind myself
I am not my mother.
Yet, I am.

I will be here when she's ready
To be healthy.
She has to want it first.

Mother's Healing

Sometimes a daughter
Has to heal
To rehabilitate her mother.

She was my daughter
Before I was hers.

منى خليل

Running

Momma woke me,
Threw me over her shoulder.
We escaped in the silence of the night.

Fearful, yet bonded,
Played out
A Lifetime movie.

My mother fought my father
So I could be free.
Today, no one fights for me
Harder than me.

بابا | Father

She sees her father.
She instantly feels the pain when looking into her eyes.
She smiles to change the emotion in her eyes.
She's made it against all odds, and she knows it.
She knows her eyes tell stories.

She knows her eyes tell stories.
She's made it against all odds, and she knows it.
She smiles to change the emotion in her eyes.
She instantly feels the pain when looking into her eyes.
She sees her father.

منى خليل

Framework

Mother told me
To marry
Someone
Who is
Evolved.

I know the moments
She shares
Shaped her
Into a million
Broken
Pieces.

HEART

منى خليل

She Said

Her last year in school
Was fifth grade.
She was twelve years old.

She was married at sixteen,
Living in a house with her mother-in-law.
The women didn't get along, but his mother chose her.
She thought about leaving her new husband.

She did not want to get married.
They met on their wedding day.

He thought she needed
Time to adjust.
He gave her
Free range.

Twenty-five years of marriage and counting.

15

منى خليل

He Said

I care about her
As the mother of our children
And my wife.

She only married me
To appease her father.
That's when it all changed.

Women aren't like men.
If they don't choose you,
They won't make the marriage work—
Not the way a man can.

I don't feel anything for her.
She does not know.

As a child,
Girls older than me
Would invite me over.

They would give me money
Or a pack of cookies
To keep me silent.

The girls instructed me
Where to put my body parts.
I learned to enjoy it.

The women I loved
Are married with
Children now.

By no means
Does one forget
The first person
They slept with.

Men want women
To hold them
In their memories.

First Love

The first boys to
Befriend me were
Black or Mexican.

The first boy
Who loved me
Was both.

منى خليل

Canvas Unclothed

Love. Her.
As. She. Is.

Dark. Hair.
Framing. Her. Face.

Goddess. Given. Brown. Skin.
Features. Curves. And. Waves.

First. Born. American.
Raised. Across. Countries.

Pronounces. Syllables. And. Accents.
Recites. Scripture. And. Hip. Hop. Lyrics.
Poetry. In. Motion.

Say. Her. Name. Right.
'Cause. She. Ain't. Becky.

منى خليل

Check Out My Melody

Love me with my flaws.
Love me with my past.
Love me whole.

To love me is to know me.

Know my spirit.
Know my intention.
Know my passion.

To know me is to feel me.

Feel my words.
Feel my confidence.
Feel my drive.

To feel me is to study me.

Hold me like a book
You can't live without.

Authentic

"If you really love somebody,
Then let them go," she said.

He said, "I'm with it. Handle yours.
When you come back to the United States,
I hope you and I can continue to grow in
honesty and openness together."

"I visited with blessings on my mind;
I came back the same.
You know where I stand as far as my feelings for you.
Don't worry—I won't ask you to wait for me.
I won't wait for you."

"I don't have to let you know
I would travel the world
Just to connect with your soul.
I would drop any girl around me for you."

"I'm gonna do my thing, just as I know you'll do yours.
That's why I asked you on the rooftop,
Instead of trying to capture your heart, to think of me."

منى خليل

Damage

As she cut him
With her words,
She cut herself—
Self-sabotage.

Be You

To be your best self,
There are no days off.

"The only way this will work
Is if you love me
From your core,"
I said.

"To love and be loved
Is not for the weak-hearted,"
I said.

He held me and said,
"Let me love you."

With Him

She saw
Her father
In him.

Cigarette-smoking
Immigrant from the Arab world.

Parents and siblings
Left behind,
He started American living.

He asked for more time.
She wasn't open.

He walked her to her car,
Watched as she drove away.
She did not look back.

Putting her on a pedestal,
He said he'd do anything
To make it work.

She saw
Her father
In him.

Thoughts of بابا's journey,
Meeting the woman who birthed her,
The connection drew her in.

It's the love story
She was reliving
With him.

منى خليل

Revelation

They told her,
"Cover your breasts."
She discovered her beauty
By how men experienced her.

دينٌ | Faith

Connecting to a higher power
In solitude.
Nobody's business.

She thought professing
Would get her closer to God.
It did the opposite.

Loving a man
Of any دينٍ
To raise children
With all the creators in the room.

Intimacy.
He holds her hand
Consistently.

She wraps her fidelity in him
As he wraps his conviction in her.

She knows the difference
Between investing
And engaging company.

She trusts
As she falls.
This could all be in her head.
What if this time is different?

منى خليل

Mr. Dark and Handsome

We appreciate the depth
In each other's
Brown-sugar glazed features.

Arched back,
Pulled hair
Leave you wondering.

He stayed up with you
Until 3:00 a.m.,
Talking.

Jasmine green tea,
Lavender honey.

At the end of the night,
You asked him if he's enjoying himself.
He said, "Of course I am."

That's the moment
You realized the real question.

"Are you enjoying yourself?"

منى خليل

Multiple

She dated two men before,
They knew.

She chose
The wrong one.
The other injured.
Here she is anew.

This time he is
Dating others.
She coerced herself
To do the same.

What if she falls for
The wrong one?
What if someone worth it all
Is buried in the rubble?

She prefers
To not be involved
With multiple people.

She picked
The wrong one again.

Morning After

I lay in my
Bed of silence.
Images of you
Mar my mind.

I let myself go
To navigate
Through affection.

I waited for you
To come after I
Cooked you dinner.
My first time.

It was lonely.
Pit in my stomach
Told me you were
With another.

We spoke for hours.
I asked you to be honest.
"Are you dating someone else?"

You said, "As of two or three weeks ago, yes."
I was hoping
I was enough.

Attraction, compatibility, and values—
You said I ran across all three.
Let's see where this leads me.

منى خليل

My glass walls,
My openness,
Intuition to safety.
Can I honestly trust you?

If only being with me
Is a place you can't get to,
Then staying won't last.

The moment I should have
Ended it—
I remember it
Perfectly.

منى خليل

Say It

Sex gave her a freedom
Of her sexuality.
He grabbed her hips,
Caressed her curves,
Relished her a**.

She convinced herself
His touch was his way
Of calling her beautiful,
Since he stopped saying it.

منى خليل

Sweet Awakening

I dreamt of you last night,
My first night in a while
Without God's name
Around my collar as I slept.

You were rubbing my back.
Your fingertips were warm oil.
It is only in the fantasy world
You are delicate with me.

منى خليل

Lion's Bait

He cared more about
The car he drove
And how he smelled
Than how he felt.

He fed her lie after lie,
Baited her in.
Started as a communicator,
Turned language of touch.

Her body became something
To be conquered.

She avoided men
Who thought of her as exotic,
Not knowing her own kind
Desire her too.

He fed her truth after truth,
Observed her well in silence.

Didn't agree with her
Massages by men,
Women seeing her flower
When honey wax meets pedals.

Little did he know
It took her years
To have custody of her body.

He voraciously ate
Her carcass
And spit her out.

To the Left

I lost my integrity
For a minute.
I wanted it back.

Hunger to move
Devotion forward.

Without realizing
He is replaceable.
I am love.

منى خليل

Mourning Loss

Feeding from my apple tree,
Stem marinating in distress,
I have hurt men.

They thirst for revenge.
He yearned to
Grudge **** me.

He said, "Just because I was upset with you
Doesn't mean I've forgotten who you are,
What we shared, and that I love you."

"Just because you hurt me, doesn't mean
I should change who I am just to 'get even'."

"I enjoyed your company.
I had a lot of emotions running through me."

He told me he spent many nights
Stewing in anger
About me abandoning him.

Vexed blame,
My newfound boundaries.

I aspire a man
Who doesn't abuse
What he reaches to keep.

Who hurt you?

منى خليل

I put down my armor,
Relaxed my muscles,
And went to sleep.

I let go of him
Like a child does a balloon.

منى خليل

Forward

Why hurt someone
Who guides you
To your own light,
Someone who helps you
Be the higher you?

My rays shine;
You try to
Damage me.

Use my energy to execute
Rather than recover.

منى خليل

Disappear

One minute you're present;
The next minute you're illusive.
Sacrifice can mean being apart.
I've mastered it.

Your sorrow
Suffocating my throat,
You never valued me.

منى خليل

Mr. Intentional

To the men
Who did not
Let me in,

Men without
Dedication
To make it work,

Men not willing to give
What they push
To get,

When time or distance
Was not on our side,
Their effort
Mediocre.

Even when I fought
To stay,
In the end
I left.

I know
When I deserve
More
Than what is being
Served at the table.

منى خليل

Challenge

She has pushed away
Every man,
Including her father.

She isn't willing to accept a partnership
Without paying attention to the etched details.
She refuses to be passive.

Newborns come into this world
Unguarded.
She parented herself.

She confronts love
With a shield
In one hand,
Sword in the other.

At what age did you learn
To guard yourself for survival?

How many times did you
Think it was safe?
Put down your defense.

Beaten down,
How are you soft?

منى خليل

إنْ شاءَ اللّه | God Willing

His name draws me in.
I have never met another.

Can my love penetrate?
Do I long to love on every level?

It is in my blood
To love you deeply.
Where has it truly led me?
Why can't I see myself?

Time could have broken us.
Reciprocity has kept us here
Throughout the years.

As I walk with courage,
I create gardens where
Nobody can hurt me.

إنْ شاءَ اللّه, you will think of me,
Recall the stroke of my
Alluring eyes.

Peace and blessings upon him
Who has hurt me
And whom I have hurt.

Us

Did I start to push him away
Before I saw red flags?
Could it be I stopped caring
Because I never actually started?

When I visualize it,
I see him standing by my side,
Interacting with my family
Wholeheartedly,

Comfortable with the idea of it all.

To be authentic, yet committed,
If he exists,
Bless me now.

منى خليل

Going

It's been years since I've dated.
I stand here debating
Whether to let you in.

Or should I hold you at a distance,
Praying everyday for clarity and guidance?
Can we get close
Without hurting each other?

Can we only get to love
If we ration
Equal risk?

My faith is strong,
But my heart is weak.
There are warriors in my chest,
Fighting a never ending battle.

Retrospect

The men
She was intimate with,
She could not trust.

She stopped entertaining
Present absent company.

Unapologetic

Don't apologize for asking him
To build a relationship,
As an active partner.
You are worth time, attention, and energy.

The work you have done on yourself
To get here.
He is pursuing you;
You are not pursuing him.

Started as a child,
When you were not in your control,
Confined by the people
Who claimed to love you.

It took you years.
A lot of time spent digging,
You had to let family know
You excavate your gold mine.

Men tell you
Proving yourself to them
Is how you win their love.

So you work and prioritize—
Tireless rollercoaster ride.
In the end, they are selfish.
You get off.

Why aren't you pursuing him?
The start is not one person
Proving their worth to someone self-anointed.

The beginning is about building a foundation,

A mutual respect,
Effortlessly.

Gravity pulling you in
Before you have to put in the work
To make it work.

You are worth pursuing,
Your love unmatched.

You did not get it for free;
Why should he?

Remind yourself
The work you did
To get here.
You are self-revelation.

WORK, WORK, WORK

Peace of Mind

Pave my own roads.
Make my own routes.
Navigation is my gift.
Problem solving my way through.

Clarity through 10,000 hours of practice,
Perseverance, and resilience,
I pursue passions.

I detach from people,
Attach to love.

Unbreakable

Cracking open
Cycles like coconuts.

To write is to exhale,
Determined to annihilate chains.

They see your vulnerability,
Say you are weak.

They will undoubtedly
Try to own you.

Drowning

Broke—
I can't tell a soul.
Mother always said, "I'd help you if I could."

منى خليل

Silver Lining

Brown girls
Don't make it
Out of these streets
Untouched,
Coming up in America
Unscathed.

They put in 1 percent,
Yet you are expected to give 99.
I keep it 100.

They have lit a fire in us.
There is no turning back from.

Tell us to prove our worth,
Fighting our way through,
Exhausted.

Challenge to challenge,
At no time have I been
Offered anything
On a silver platter.
Have you?

Miracles

Work hard
When you're
Envisioning.

Vision is work.

Nah

Try to control me.
Tell me to work harder,
Smile more,
Sacrifice my time and family.

Knowing you don't give a sh** about me,
I must make you feel comfortable.

Otherwise I don't fit in
Organizational culture.

I am one of few shades of brown.
To be unsatisfied here,
To them it means,
There is something wrong with me.

I can't walk in and be myself.
I have to remind myself,
Not to be myself.

Realizing I am truly
Not welcomed
In this community.

Cheap labor—
Positioned to be less
Than those around me.
How did I get here again?

Never trust anyone
Who tells you
You are not worth
What you have worked for.

Ellipses

Do you crave
More for yourself
Than anyone can imagine?

How does it feel
To put in work
And not have
Financial stability
Or recognition
To show for it?

Fighting for what
You have built
Inside you.

Feeling like everything
You have accomplished
A prerequisite.

Check your paycheck.
You are worth more.
You always will be.

You had to learn quickly.
Rest only comes in safe spaces.

You are saving your sanity
In the most natural way.

Red, White, and Blue

America promotes their work,
After their death.
Without recognizing the agony it inflicted;
Robbed them of
Freedom, faith, and dignity.

They publicize,
Speaking up as anti-American.
Disgracing our humility
Is anti-American.

Born and raised in America,
Brown and Muslim in America,
Mixed race growing up in America,
Arab, Black, Latina in America,

Indigenous people of America,
Immigrants and refugees
Built a home in America,
All laid the bricks of America.

America made us through our
Hardships and lessons,
Learning resilience through America's beatings.

Treated as less than
Rockets' red glare,
Bombs bursting in air,
Whiteness is a currency.

America taught me spirituality and sexuality,
Make people uncomfortable,
Less open to human beings.

منى خليل

America made me unlearn
And learn I am more,
Suppressing me, glorified me.
I am greatness.

PROSPERITY

منى خليل

Counsel of Women

Natural hair,
Deep skin,
You are the definition of beauty.

Women who use
Their body as a profession,
Hands to heal,
Mouth to thread.

Families you create,
Experiencing languages across continents.
You are the definition of superpower.

To the women who welcome me
Into their imperfect world,
Aroma of spice trade
Through their kitchen,

You cook for hours with your bare hands.
You've made hundreds of meals,
Fed thousands of people.
Our stomachs tell stories of you.

Thank you to the women who welcome me in,
A guest in each of their hearts,
Vulnerable force at our core.
We connect effervescently.

Note to Self

Protect your warmth.
Invest in yourself.
Focus.

Every state is a layover.
Lucky you to be traveling,
Obtaining more for yourself.

Grow in opportunity,
Perseverance in challenge,
Gratitude in every goal achieved.

منى خليل

Wanderer

You can't deceive
What you lack
In growth
Unveiled
Through decisions.

Don't neglect
Watering yourself;
You are the soil
Food grows from.

Reminds me of my parents
Pulling me by my limbs,
People stretching me.

If I gave each person I adore
The time they ask of me,
I would do nothing for myself.

That's how it all started.

I made myself available
to everyone,
Making each of them
Feel as special as they are.

One day I took it all away.
I moved to Africa,
Hid in the pockets of Morocco,
As I do in America today.

منى خليل

Do you not understand
There are more of you than me?
Boundaries became a necessity
For my loyalty and love.

I've made wrong turns.
I've made right ones too.
What I will never do
Is stop embodying truth.

How do you treat a bird
That keeps flying back?
Do you feed it
Or let it fly away?

Egyptian Phoenix

Stories untold,
They knock her on
Cemented ground.

She screams
From the insides
Of her lungs.

When flame meets fire,
They burn her awake,
Scar her.

Rising phoenix,
Ashes to dust,
Wings unclipped.

Her voyage,
Tunnel after tunnel
Within.

She has so much
To be grateful for.

She buries people
Deep in the sand
Of her memory.

Future State

Life is about shooting threes,
Exceeding to new heights,
Present with the man
I name husband.

My next job, my career:
Centering myself,
Always choosing my soul.

EPILOGUE

(Mona Khalil, sixteen years old)

Love is a struggle to find.
Youth do not keep an open mind.
With doubt in their heart,
"Love" they speak.
This is a sign of you being weak.

Young adults yearn
To feel the experience too,
But don't allow their heart to be true.
Don't you understand love is above all?
Why can't you wait for its call?

Love is a feeling that does not go away.
With the loving embrace of two,
The ones who truly feel it are very few.

Some bind together in love,
Divorce, and it's through.
This is an example
Of your heart not being true.

You say you love one
And love another the same.
Love is not that weak;
It is only one's gain.

You should open your heart.
Now take a deep breath.
Allow that question to lie on your chest.

First find yourself.
Allow another to wait.
Trust me—when he does,
He will pass through
A loving open gate.